Hidden Treasures

Revealing What Life's Been Concealing

Hidden Treasures

Revealing What Life's Been Concealing

Michelle Beckett

Published by Truth2RenewHearts Publishing
An imprint of Truth2RenewHearts Enterprises, LLC
Pittsburgh, Pennsylvania

For information:
Info@truth2renewheartspublishing.com

ISBN-13: 978-0-9864482-3-2
ISBN-10: 0-9864482-3-0

Cover design by Robin Miller

Unless otherwise indicated, Scripture quotations are from:
The Holy Bible, King James Version, New King James Version

Dedication

This book is dedicated to the memory of my Father, the late Elder Robert L. Beckett Sr. Thank you for the love, life lessons, and the smiles you brought to my life. I will love and miss you forever Daddy.

I also dedicate this book to every woman who has a deep desire to find out what they were created for. To every woman who has a desire to do an amazing work for the Lord, but you're not sure where to start. It is your time to activate your gifts so you can walk in purpose. I pray this book is the launching pad to reveal every hidden treasure in your life.

Contents

Foreword

Our trials and experiences help mold us into the women of purpose God intends for us to be. While in the midst of a storm, it can be very difficult to discern that the tribulations in your life can also turn out to be your greatest treasures.

As Michelle shares her good *and* adverse experiences, this transparent literary work gives you a glimpse into her life, while prompting you to take inventory of your own hopes, dreams, and unanswered questions. While reading this book, you will understand that your trials propel you into the greatest triumphs of your journey. In addition to providing guidance and spiritual wisdom, this book also serves as a life raft to those who feel that they are drowning in a sea of discouragement. Upon digging into each chapter, you will be uplifted, encouraged, and your hope will be restored as Michelle coaches you to victory.

If you have ever struggled with fulfilling your purpose or questioned God about why you had to endure harsh experiences with no clear explanation, then this book is for you.

I encourage you to sit down with this book, carve out some time for yourself, and keep a pen and paper on hand for making notes.

I am very proud of the woman of God that Michelle Beckett has become and I am ecstatic about her future. I know that your future will shine bright as you infuse the principles of this book into your life, while allowing God to reveal unto you what life has attempted to conceal.

Evangelist Yvette D. Thoroughgood, LPN
Pastor of Women's Ministry
Church of the Advent COGIC

Introduction

Have you ever wondered why you were created? Are you struggling to identify your divine purpose here on earth? Do you spend countless hours thinking, *"There must be more to me than this"*? Do you often wonder, *"What can I do for the Kingdom of God?"*

If you've been asking yourself any of these questions, this book is for you. Until I discovered my purpose, I spent numerous days, hours, and even years pondering those same questions. I often felt like God forgot to give me something special to do. However, today I am thrilled to say that I am glorifying Him with my gifts and walking boldly in my purpose and you can do the same.

I am inviting you on the journey to discovering *your* purpose and your hidden treasures. As you read this book, I will be walking with you every step of the way. While encouraging and empowering you, I will also share my personal journey to discovering my purpose and the hidden treasure inside of me. It is my prayer that you read this book with an open heart and mind so that you can receive all that God has in store for you throughout this process. Let the purpose party begin!

CHAPTER 1

Welcome to the Reveal Party

To be very honest with you, so many negative things had occurred in my childhood and adult life that I felt like I didn't have any treasures. My circumstances led me to believe that I had nothing to give anyone, however, I could not have been any more wrong. God surely created and formed me with great purpose. I let life conceal what heaven was trying to reveal in me. Maybe you have felt the same way. You are probably like I was and you have lots of hidden treasures inside of you waiting to be unleashed!

What are hidden treasures? Hidden treasures are gifts, talents, and purpose that is inside of us that we have not yet identified. Quite often, we can better identify the treasures within other people before we recognize our own. If you've spent any amount of time in church, I'm sure you can identify with gifts such as preaching, teaching, evangelism, and singing. These are visible gifts that usually put those who possess them in the "spotlight". Those individuals are usually in the public eye and often in leadership roles throughout our churches.

While the more public gifts are amazing and wonderful, there are so many other gifts and purposes in the Body of Christ that help to make up the Kingdom of God. All gifts are given by God, for the purpose of God to be fulfilled through us.

II Corinthians 4:7 says, "But we have this treasure in earthen vessels that the excellency of the power may be of God, and not of us". The vessels the scripture is referring to are *us*! The gifts inside of us are for no other reason than to display God's power. God wants to use us in the earth and has placed treasures inside of us for His glory.

Hidden treasures are buried treasures that require concentrated effort to find them. When you search for buried treasures, you must stay focused and you must have a strategic plan in order to find what you are looking for. For example, when people are looking for hidden treasures such as gold while at the beach, they don't waste time looking for other objects. They know the buried treasure is often found under a lot of debris, so that's where they spend time their time looking.

Hidden treasures may be hidden from you for a period of time for a variety of reasons. Some treasures cannot be revealed and released until you undergo a process of maturation. Maturity is necessary so that specific treasures are not misused. In addition, living a lifestyle of sin can keep you from discovering your hidden treasures. Treasures may also be hidden for a period of time unbeknownst to us, simply because God's ways and thoughts are higher than ours. God knows the best time to reveal the hidden treasures in your life. In some cases, hidden treasures can be unfounded because we do not take the time to invest in our relationship with God. Keep in mind, no matter the number of treasures you possess, only the Master knows *how* He wants the treasures to be shared in the earth. In other words, God has the blueprint, He knows the intent of the treasure, and He knows when and where it will have the greatest impact. This is why a personal *relationship* with God is vital in this process.

There is no such thing as a gift or treasure too big or too small, because all are needed. Everyone in the earth has a purpose for which they are created. In order to recognize our purpose, we first have to understand who we are.

My Struggles

My struggle with purpose began while growing up in church. I seemingly had no visible talents or purpose. I sang in the choir but was not a soloist. I could simply carry a tune and note when I was directed to. I felt like there was nothing significant about my voice. I grew up with friends in church who could *really* sing. Their voices were out of this world. One of my friends is actually a national recording artist!

In addition, when it came to speaking, I was very shy and self-conscious, so I could not bear to be up in front of people and actually speak out. I lacked the confidence to be considered any kind of speaker. I knew the word of God, but again I felt there was nothing significant about my voice.

I began to compare myself to others around me. I didn't realize that comparison was the thief of joy and contentment. I saw myself through the eyes of how I thought others saw me.

I started to question how God could love me and seemingly forget to give me anything special. At a young age, I began to feel that God loved me and tolerated me, but maybe He didn't like me. Because of this, I started not to like myself either.

I was engulfed with feelings of worthlessness. I allowed low self-esteem, feeling unloved, rejection, defeat, feeling ugly, and much more, control my life. These inner feelings plagued me for so many years. I allowed these negative feelings to dictate my life and my responses to life's issues and circumstances.

My relationship with God was up and down. Can you imagine fully serving and loving a God who you didn't feel like cared about you too much? It made my journey very difficult. I wanted to be saved and live a Christian life, so I did, but I always questioned how God felt about me. I began to weigh all the bad things that occurred in my life and always came to the conclusion that God didn't love me or He wasn't too pleased with me. I later found out that this was not true!

Knowing the Word of God and *applying* the Word of God are two very different things. I read the Bible, memorized lots of scriptures, I quoted scriptures, but I didn't believe that they really applied to me; especially if it was good. What a sad mindset to live by.

Let's face it, life has happened to all of us. The good, the bad, and the ugly. Life's circumstances and issues can either propel you to walk in purpose, or they can cripple you to the point of being stagnant.

The Truth

I want you to know that you are a woman of purpose. I don't care what you have encountered in life, no matter how many losses, failures, setbacks and disappointments you have lived through, God still has purpose for you.

You really have to understand your importance in the Kingdom of God. You and I are part of God's Kingdom. We are God's ambassadors here in the earth.

Treasures are for NOW! Treasures are to be used here on earth. They are not transferable. We must work while it is day. We must share the word of God and the love of God through what He has deposited in us. There is no need to store them up for later, we must use them now.

We do not have time to waste what God has deposited in us. Can you imagine standing before God and He shows you all that you were supposed to do but didn't do? I don't know about you, but I don't want that to happen to me. I want to stand before God in peace, knowing that everything He put inside of me, I used it in His honor, so that He may be glorified.

No matter what your treasures are, your gifts are significant and specifically designed for the people you have been called to. Yes, I said *called* to. We are all called to minister and impact certain people here in the earth. God orchestrates this through our connections with our family, friends, co-workers, affiliations, neighborhood, churches, and other entities we are a part of. God uses your connections for His glory. You are connected to specific people for specific reasons. Perhaps you have convinced yourself that you should play the supporting role to others. There is nothing wrong with helping others as they advance the Kingdom. However, sometimes people tend to hide behind others, and never tap into or develop what God has given them. If this is you and you have the ministry of helps, I want you to know that there are additional treasures inside of you that God wants to reveal for His glory. It is perfectly fine to support others, but you have a purpose and a destiny too!

The Reveal

You may be asking, "What is the big reveal?" The big reveal is that you are a woman of purpose, full of hidden treasures that need to be shared with the world.

Embrace it. I am talking to you. Yes, you! You are here on assignment and you have work to do. Someone is waiting for an encounter with you. You have what they need in order to propel them to their next level, to propel them to their greater destiny, and to thrust them into purpose.

God has a purpose and a plan for each and every one of us. Jeremiah 29:11 declares, "For I know the thoughts I think toward you, saith the Lord, thoughts of peace, and not of evil, to give you an expected end". God not only loves us, but He also thinks good thoughts toward us. Growing up, I don't recall hearing this scripture and, if I did, it was not one I could remember until much later in life.

I will discuss the importance of knowing God's Word later in the book.

It was my discontentment with my life that led me to purpose. I always knew that there had to be more, but for so many years I did not consider myself worthy of purpose.

As I matured, I started to develop a relationship with God. From this relationship with God, I began to sense that there was more to life than me going to work, going to church, and raising my son.

In certain settings, I began to hear the word *purpose*. Oh, I had been in services where I listened to the word *purpose* come from the preacher's mouth countless times, but this was the first time I actually *heard* "purpose" and thought of myself! My interest was sparked and I began to read more about purpose, gifts, and callings. Once I began the process of discovering my purpose, it led me on the journey to discovering my true and authentic self too. Over time, I realized that God had not forgotten me, that He loved me, and He was working in my life along. I even became aware that I was actually in alignment with purpose in ways I hadn't recognized before.

Once I became open to having purpose, God allowed me to be exposed to different people and venues and my treasures were suddenly revealed.

Today I am a woman walking in purpose and I know my worth and recognize my treasures. I am thrilled that I can boldly and confidently say this now and I pray you will experience this same joy very soon!

Prayer

"Lord, open my eyes so that I may see all that you are going to reveal to me. I accept that I do have purpose and hidden treasures and with your help, I will walk in them boldly and confidently! Amen."

CHAPTER 2

Life Happens

Let's face it. Life has happened to all us. The plans we have go awry. We experience unexpected losses, hurts, disappointments, failures, sickness, and the list goes on. If you have been in the world for any amount of time, you have experienced what we call life.

Even the best laid plans and goals we set for ourselves are no match for life. Life happens when we are prepared and when we are not prepared. Life continues even after death.

Survival Mode

Sometimes when many things are bombarding us at one time, we can go into survival mode. Survival mode occurs when you do what you need to do in order to make it each day. Survival mode does not really allow much time to dream and plan. All of your energy and focus is on "making it".

I found myself living like this, however, I didn't realize it until I was 20 years in. I also found myself a divorced single parent. I was working, but I didn't make a whole lot of money. My credit was not good. I was struggling to make ends meet on a daily basis. Doors I thought would have provided an opportunity to improve my station in life, were closed before my eyes. I was in a cycle of depression, failure, and hopelessness. I would have never said this then, but I can admit it now; I was severely depressed most of my adult life. Most people who know me will attest to that fact that they had no idea that I was depressed because I covered it up very well.

I remember standing in my kitchen on my 29th birthday after opening my mail and seeing yet another loss on paper. As I was depressed, hopeless and tired, for the second time in my life, I considered suicide. I remember looking at the knife and thinking I should end it all and put myself out of misery. I didn't attempt suicide because I started thinking about the fact that it would hurt my mother. I didn't even consider my son, because I honestly thought he would be better off without me. I thought about the consequences of taking my own life. The despair was overwhelming at that moment. I can't tell you anything significant happened, but those thoughts of suicide passed, and deep inside, I was given a nudge to go on a little further. I know now that it was the Holy Spirit who encouraged me not to give up. I am forever grateful to God that He saved my life yet again.

Life Happens to Children Too

At the tender age of 12, I recall the *first* time I considered suicide. I tried to commit suicide by taking a number of pills. I don't remember what kind of pills they were, but I know that after taking a handful of them, I fell asleep. Had it not been for God, that could have been the end of me. I woke up disoriented, but fine. I thank God for His hand of protection on me.

Perhaps you are wondering why a 12-year-old would be at the point of suicide. Let me tell you how I got to that point.

The first time I started to feel like something was wrong with me was in Kindergarten. Prior to Kindergarten, I was the baby of a large blended family. My Mom and I spent our days together while everyone else was in school. She taught me to read and write. I felt loved, spoiled, and special.

I was very outgoing and confident, however, once I got to school, there was a difference; I was bigger than the other girls. My teeth were big and gapped. The teasing started. In the beginning, I brushed it off, but as time went on I began to believe that what was being said about me was true. This pattern continued throughout elementary school. As I got older, I covered up my hurt by using my own sharp mouth and sense humor to take shots at others before they were taken at me. For years, I continued to combat the hurt and rejection that I felt in this way.

Somewhere between the ages of nine and eleven, I experienced molestation at the hands of a close family member. The things that I was exposed to, no child should be exposed to. This began to validate that something was wrong with me and that no one seemed to like me in public, but only behind closed doors. This molestation set the stage in my adult life to settling for whatever was being offered.

In middle school, I was constantly ridiculed and made fun of. I was an oddball because growing up in the Pentecostal "sanctified" church we did not wear pants, so I stood out in another way. I was chubby, had a large gap in my front teeth, *and* felt unpretty. In high school, the teasing continued, but it wasn't as severe as what took place in middle school. However, I still saw the difference between me and the other girls. It seemed every friend I had was a "normal" girl who had relationships with different guys, but I never had a boyfriend in school. I continued to hate myself because the boys didn't like me. Again, life was happening and I felt like I was drowning.

In church, I felt the same rejection on a somewhat different level. I was a part of all the different things available to the youth: the choir, the usher board, and the step team. I went to a church where most of the folks there were related to at least one or two other families in the church. This made me feel like an outsider. I was part of the various auxiliaries, but there was nothing significant about me. I was always in the background. I could not sing, I was too shy and self-conscious to be out front, and I just didn't feel like I had anything going for me.

These are just some of the childhood and teenage experiences that contributed to shaping me into a negative, self-conscious, low self- esteem young lady. Life was happening to me, and I was not winning.

Due to the things that were happening to me, I felt like God must favor other people more than me. I wondered why He allowed me to look the way I did, to be treated the way I was, and I wondered why He didn't endow me with special gifts or talents. My negative experiences caused me to misinterpret who God really was. Certainly, He couldn't love me and allow me to experience all that I experienced? Surely not.

I can say at different times in my life I was angry with God. Harboring anger in your soul conceals the goodness in life. I felt that if He loved me, He wouldn't allow all of the hurt and pain. I felt at one point, God created me to be a failure. Yes, I said a failure. The enemy not only talked to my mind, he had me believing that God didn't love or like me and that God wanted me to be hurt for one reason or another. Because of this, for a long while, I wasn't able to see the good things that God *was* doing in my life.

While growing up, I was also dealing with a non-existent relationship with my Dad. I grew up with him in the home, but we did not have a good relationship at all. I will tell you that at the age of 41, God gave me my heart's desire and allowed me to become a "Daddy's girl". From the time he was diagnosed with a Stage IV Glioblastoma, until hours before he took his last breath, God allowed me to be there every step of the way. I was a Daddy's girl all the way until my Dad passed on October 18, 2017. God gave me glorious years that made up for all the distance, misunderstandings, and hurts. I type this with tears because I miss my Dad. I am so grateful to God for what He did for us. When God does a thing, He knows how to erase the bad and make it all good.

At the time I didn't realize that through my lack of relationship my Dad, that God would later show me the power of reconciliation and healing. Life concealed that God could resurrect what seemed hopeless and bring much joy. His power took the sting out of the previous hurt I felt! He is just that kind of God.

The experiences in my life seem to conceal the fact that God truly cared about me, and that I was fearfully and wonderfully made. Eventually as God kept me, I emerged from these negative life experiences a confident, wise, anointed, beautiful, woman of God. I learned to look in the mirror and love who I saw staring back at me.

Young Adult Years

As I became a young adult, for a period of time I was in a backslidden state. I spent my weekends clubbing and doing things I had no business doing, looking for love in all the wrong places. Remember, I was a broken little girl that became a broken young lady who did not understand the love of God, nor understand my earthly Father.

I didn't last too long in that clubbing lifestyle, it simply wasn't me. Soon after, I got saved, got back in church and met my future ex-husband. Then, I became pregnant.

Ironically, I didn't get pregnant while I was out partying. I got back in church and got pregnant at the age of 22! When this happened, I felt the sequence of events in my life were backwards. My ex-husband and I married six months after our son was born. I will just say that if I didn't have low self- esteem and was not as broken as I was, then I would not have entertained this relationship. I was looking for love when I didn't really love myself. There were other issues too, but I will not address those at this time. Needless to say, the marriage did not last, and in under two years, I was separated and had to adjust to life as a single parent. The loss of this dysfunctional marriage further solidified in my mind that something must be wrong with me. Plus, going through a divorce when the two of us went to the same church, was not easy. It was hard for us to both continue in the same ministry, so my ex-husband eventually left the ministry. I was riddled with guilt about going through a divorce. Christians don't divorce right? Wrong! Life happens.

It has only been because of my experiences of going through an out of wedlock pregnancy and a subsequent divorce, that God has now allowed me to counsel and coach others experiencing the same things. My wonderful son was born in 1994. He is a bright and wonderful young man. I am thankful for him. The struggle became real when around the age of four, we discovered that he had a developmental delay disability. I was devastated. I began to take on the guilt of him having a learning disability. I thought maybe God was punishing me because he was born out of wedlock. I was in survival mode, dealing with depression, the breakup of my marriage, and now my son has a learning disability? I had to work and could not be home with him. I carried guilt about him having a learning disability. I carried guilt about not being able to be at home to really help him. My son spent his school years being in self-contained classes for the majority of the time, and as he entered high school, he also entered some of the mainstream classes. I really didn't know how to help him. The people I reached out to offered no solutions. He graduated high school and was accepted into a community college. The struggle has been great, but he is currently in school and working part time. He is even a licensed minister. Most of all, he is a warm, kind, loving young man who is liked by many and He is a true man of God. I couldn't be more proud of the man he is today.

I allowed the struggles that I had with my son's learning disability, and lack of finances to do for him as I desired conceal the fact that God entrusted me to raise and nurture His manservant. I didn't see this while I was raising him, because all I concentrated on were the struggles.

As I mentioned, in regard to my marriage, it has only been because of my experiences of going through an out of wedlock pregnancy and a subsequent divorce, that God has now allowed me to counsel and coach others experiencing the same things in their lives.

I shared a portion of my story so that you can see how I got to the point that life concealed what Heaven was trying to reveal. I will be sharing more in the upcoming chapters. As you are reading this book, begin to reflect back on your own life. Can you see where some of your life struggles have concealed your treasures and gifts?

Are You Simply Surviving?

Survival mode is a real way of life that leaves us void of fulfilling purpose and discovering our treasures. Have you found yourself in survival mode? Perhaps you are feeling depleted, your energy drained by all that you have had to deal with. I want to encourage you to come out of survival mode and dare to dream again. Dare to believe and receive all that God has for you.

I remember years of praying prayers of repentance. I thought I had offended God. I was literally praying all the time apologizing for any offenses. I had no concept of the love of God, and the plans that He has for us. I was messed up mentally! I had no faith, and without faith it is impossible to please God. I always believed that God had all power and could do any and everything, but the question I wrestled with was, would He do it for *me*? I had no faith, and a doubting spirit.

Life's circumstances concealed the love that God had for me. Life concealed that I was worthy of love. Life concealed that I am beautiful. Life concealed that I have purpose. Life concealed that I had hidden treasures waiting to be revealed.

I want you to know that I experienced good in the midst of some bad life circumstances, even though at the time, I was dealing with life issues so I could not see any goodness. I developed life-long friendships with people from my church and school. I'm still friends with many of them today. I was blessed and didn't recognize it. I became, and still am a counselor, confidant, and coach to several of them. The same for my family. I am the person that most come to for advice, an opinion, and even for ideas. I am the person that gives encouragement and support.

Can you see how I was consumed with the problems of my life? There was no room for purpose or treasures to be revealed. Every good thing was concealed. What am I saying? Life happens to us all, maybe in different ways or areas, but it is still happening. We go into survival mode and most times we are unable to thrive because of it.

Survival mode allows us to give just what we need to give, never *reaching* for more or *giving* more of ourselves.

Even if you have been in survival mode for many years, it is time for you to thrive in all that God desires for your life. Life is going to happen; however, we must see it for what it is. Life happens, but it does not triumph over purpose. Keep in mind you've been created for a reason and purpose, and no matter what you encounter, you have destiny to fulfill. The Word of God tells us in John 10:10 "Beloved above all I would that ye prosper and be in good health, even as your soul prospers". This verse lets us know God has plans that extend way beyond survival mode.

I made the mistake that many have made, and that is coming into agreement with Satan, whom the Bible calls the "father of lies" (John 8:44). In the next chapter, I will expose the tactics of the enemy.

Treasure Tip

Some people consider taking "selfies" a habit of conceited people. For me, taking selfies allowed me to love who I saw. I began to take selfies until I loved who was staring back at me. I then gained courage to post them on social media, not for the likes, but because I liked how I looked. If you suffer from low self-esteem or a poor self- image, I encourage you to keep taking selfies until you love who you see.

Questions to Ponder

1. How have you let life conceal your treasures?
2. Have you really looked at your life's struggles in the right way?

CHAPTER 3

Concealed
Weapons

Are you armed and dangerous because you haven't been trained on the proper way to carry concealed weapons?

Concealed weapons can be good when we are properly licensed to carry them. We become licensed when we understand what God's Word says about them and when we are using them appropriately.

Perhaps you are wondering what concealed weapons are. Concealed weapons are devices that can destroy lives, but they are not easily identified by the untrained eye. Identifying concealed weapons will require a trained spiritual eye. Concealed weapons are usually within close proximity to us. These concealed weapons are so dangerous because they are not only close to us, but they have unlimited access to us because we are not aware of them.

It is such a scary thought that a weapon of mass destruction can be so close to us, have access to us, and have the ability to destroy us -if unchecked!

Tongue

The tongue is a concealed weapon. The Bible says, "Even so the tongue is a little member and boasts great things. And the tongue is a fire, a world of iniquity. The tongue is so set among our members that it defiles the whole body and sets on fire the course of nature; and it is set on fire by hell. [7] For every kind of beast and bird, of reptile and creature of the sea, is tamed and has been tamed by mankind. [8] But no man can tame the tongue. It is an unruly evil, full of deadly poison. [9] With it we bless our God and Father, and with it we curse men, who have been made in the similitude of God. [10] Out of the same mouth proceed blessing and cursing. My brethren, these things ought not to be so. [11] Does a spring send forth fresh water and bitter from the same opening? [12] Can a fig tree, my brethren, bear olives, or a grapevine bear figs? Thus no spring yields both saltwater and fresh." - James 3:5-12

The tongue is small, yet a powerful and deadly member. It resides in our body and we carry it each day. Your tongue has the power to speak blessings and it has the power to curse things. The tongue is one of the deadliest of the concealed weapons because we can speak the wrong thing out of our mouths.

Psalms 34:13 instructs us to "Keep your tongue from evil, and your lips from speaking deceit". When we don't agree with what the Word of God says, we are speaking evil. We can speak evil not only about others, but also about ourselves. This is a concealed weapon. What we say does matter. Sometimes, life and circumstances can bring us to a place where we want to murmur and complain, but when we give into it, we are speaking evil over our own lives. It is a daily practice to keep your tongue from speaking evil. Many people say whatever they want to say under the guise that they are keeping it real. Just because something may be true, it does not always need to be said. We must learn to practice the art of being quiet.

Proverbs 21:23 says, "Whoever guards his tongue keeps his soul from troubles". Keeping our tongue will keep our soul from trouble. So many negative situations arise simply because we do not keep our tongue. How much trouble could you and I have avoided if we would have guarded our tongue? Probably lots of things could have been avoided.

Many people are in a vicious cycle of trouble and life struggles simply because of their tongue. How many times have we let reckless words come out of our mouths? Have you ever uttered these words in a time of frustration, *"I am never going to get out of debt"*? Or *"I can't seem do anything right"*. *"I am never going to get what I want our life"*. Does any of this sound familiar?

In times of irritation, frustration, depression and stressful situations, it is easy to utter negative words. At the time, we just feel as if we are venting, but what we are really doing is speaking curses over our own lives. At any time, did God the Father ever say any of these things to you? I can answer that, NO! No matter what we are going through, we are to always speak the Word of God, so we position ourselves to speak positively over our situations. We can say, *"Lord, I don't have the answer to this situation. I am feeling all types of ways, but I know that you are going to bring me out some way, somehow"*. If you don't want to say that, simply speak God's Word.

For example, speak Romans 8:28 which says, "And we know that all things work together for the good of them who love the Lord and are called according to His purpose". So our response to our trouble, even in these dark circumstances would be, *I know that all things are working together for my good.*

We don't have to act as if we aren't dealing with some hard and daunting situations, but what we must do is acknowledge that our situations don't triumph over God's Word, or His promises to us. Do not be a breeding ground of negativity about your own self. Self-sabotage is horrible. It is one thing for us to encounter the harsh words of others, but imagine destroying yourself from the inside out because of what you let your tongue say.

Our words can hurt or help us. Our words can hurt or help others. Words matter! Don't be the assassin to your own destiny or the destiny of others with the words that come out of your mouth. Proverbs 18:21 declares, "Death and life are in the power of the tongue: and those that love it will eat its fruit". Choose to speak life to any and every circumstance. Choose to speak life to others. Always be a source of encouragement and peace to everyone you come in contact with. What have you spoken over your own life that didn't line up with the word of God? Ephesians 4:29 admonishes us to "Let no corrupt communication proceed out of your mouth, but that which is good to the use of edifying, that it may minister grace unto the hearers". Watch what you say!

Mind

The mind is a concealed weapon. Philippians 2:5 says, "Let this mind be in you that was also in Christ Jesus". 2 Timothy 1:7 says, "For God has not given us the spirit of fear, but of power, love, and a sound mind". The Word of God declares that God has given us a sound mind. Although God has given us a sound mind, we have to renew our minds daily. Sometimes the cares of life hit us with so many things at once, it easy to slip into a negative mind set. It is easy to come into agreement with what our circumstances are dictating. Maybe you've received a bad report from the doctor, or you are experiencing marital troubles, financial problems, opposition on the job, and the list goes on; it can be overwhelming at times if we do not renew our minds daily through prayer and the reading the word of God. We make it easy for the enemy our soul to wreak continued havoc in our lives when we come into agreement with the adverse circumstances being thrown our way.

The mind is a concealed weapon because our thoughts shape our lives. Our thoughts shape how we view things, and we can subconsciously agree with the wrong things. Our mind goes everywhere with us and it houses our thoughts. If we are not aware of this concealed weapon, we will find ourselves using it throughout the day in the wrong way.

Ephesians 4:23 says, "And be renewed in the spirit of your mind". Romans 12:2 states, "And be not conformed to this world: but be ye transformed by the renewing of your mind, that ye may prove what is that good, and acceptable, and perfect, will of God".

We are to renew our minds. What does this mean? We have to reprogram our mind to think the right things. We have to condition our mind through the reading of God's Word so that we can think on the right things. In Philippians 4:8, the Bible instructs us to think on whatever things are pure, just, of a good report, if there be any virtue or any praise, think of these things.

I will recommend reading "Battlefield of the Mind" by Joyce Meyer. It is a powerful book that shows you how to conquer the thoughts in your mind.

Heart

The heart is a concealed weapon because it can become bitter and it can hold unforgiveness, hurts, and offenses. The heart can be a heart of stone. It can become hardened and evil. Our heart posture can poison us, keeping us from recognizing any goodness that God wants to bring our way. Negative life circumstances can happen to us all. There are times that we do encounter situations where we have been used, abused, manipulated, and hurt. When our emotions are left unchecked, it leads to a bitter, broken heart.

The heart is a concealed weapon. "As a man thinketh in his heart, so is he" (Proverbs 23:7). Can you see how the thoughts we think in our heart can shape who we become? It is important to have a pure heart in all situations. A pure heart is not easy to achieve, but it can be done through humility, a willingness to forgive, and desire to please God. Remember, according to Matthew 5:8, "Blessed are the pure in heart, for they shall see God". A pure heart is a requirement to see God and to be blessed!

The condition of your heart matters. Your heart can shape your mind and thoughts, and your mind and thoughts can shape the words that you speak out of your mouth. Now do you see the importance of knowing how to properly handle these concealed weapons? They are powerful in their own individual right, but when put together, they are a deadly force that can kill the plans and desires that God has for you.

The Dangers of Mishandling Concealed Weapons

I can tell you that I have been guilty of misusing all three of these concealed weapons, because I didn't have the knowledge of what I was doing and saying in my own life. I have spoken so many negative words in my life over the years because I didn't realize the effect of my words. I felt that my thoughts were private and didn't have anything to do with what was going on in my life. At one point, my heart became bitter and I carried a lot of anger toward God. I believed that God didn't really love me, I allowed the enemy to convince me that God enjoyed my pain. Imagine that! I was convinced at one point of my life that God somehow took pleasure in my hurts and pains, which was why He didn't do anything about the things that I was dealing with.

Improper use of my concealed weapons, were killing me softly. Between my tongue, my mind, and my heart, I became my own worst enemy. Life was happening as it should, but I added so much more to the experiences.

When our tongue, minds, and hearts come into agreement with the enemy we become poison to our souls. I know that these concealed weapons are powerful because they choked the life out me. My faith was almost non-existent, I didn't believe any good was coming to me.

We all know without faith it is impossible to please God. I was not pleasing to God, because I allowed my concealed weapons to be unleashed in my life in such a negative way.

Be careful, because if you ever get to this state, you can take on a victim mentality. The victim mentality will have you believing that you are all alone in the things you are dealing with. It can convince you that no one understands you because what you are going through is greater than what another person has ever encountered. Understand that we all go through various trials and tribulations. Even if the people in your inner circle have not encountered the exact things you are facing, know that they are fighting their own battles and dealing with their own issues too. No one is exempt from life!

I wanted to expose these concealed weapons because they are a part of us and we carry them daily with us. When these concealed weapons are not exposed, they can lead us to coming into agreement with negative things, things that God has not said about us.

Consider this, concealed weapons can be used for good. We have exposed the negative effects of being improperly trained to use concealed weapons. Now let's discuss the benefits of concealed weapons.

How can concealed weapons be used for good? By thinking good thoughts about ourselves, our lives, and the plans God has for us. Jeremiah 29:11 reminds us of God's plan, "For I know the thoughts that I think toward you, saith the LORD, thoughts of peace, and not of evil, to give you an expected end".

When was the last time you looked in the mirror and saw something good staring back at you? When was the last time you encouraged yourself? When was the last time you loved on yourself flaws and all? We have to speak life over us daily. Tell yourself how wonderful you are, remember how far you've come, recall who you used to be while thanking God for progress, and tell yourself you will walk in destiny and purpose. Sometimes we are encouragers and motivators to others but we forget about ourselves. You are amazing, don't you know that? After all the things you have been through, you are still here, still in the fight, and that is amazing!

We are required to have a pure heart. One cannot keep a pure heart when harboring unforgiveness. We can keep our heart pure by quickly releasing offenses, forgiving those who may have hurt us, and letting go of rejection and hurts. Forgiveness is a choice. We make the choice to harbor offenses. We decide if we are going to forgive the individual who hurt us or if we are going to hold a grudge. How many times have you harbored in your heart painful memories, painful betrayals, and painful situations and have yet to release them?

Ask yourself the hard question, "Why am I holding onto this offense?" Perhaps you are waiting an acknowledgement of wrongdoing? Maybe you are waiting on an apology you may never get. Do you want revenge or justice served on the person or persons who wounded you? Forgiveness is not for the other person, it is for you, so that you keep your heart pure before the Lord. Forgiveness does not mean you to allow that person to be in your personal space, but it does mean you release them from the offense so you can earnestly love them and pray for them with no malice in your heart. It is a tall order, but our Lord requires us to forgive and to love.

Speak well of God, speak well of others, speak well of yourself. Speak life, give encouragement, show love, speak faith, speak hope, be a life giver through your words.

Proper use of concealed weapons lets God know that we believe His word and that we believe in what He has promised us through His word. It releases our faith. It helps our unbelief. It shows God that we trust Him even when we don't see how the way will be made and can't even imagine how our deliverance will come.

Now that the light of exposure has been shined on concealed weapons, how will you carry them going forward? The choice of life and death lies within you.

Questions to Ponder

1. Have you become a danger to yourself by incorrectly using your concealed weapons?
2. Have you been firing shots and sabotaging your own life by using concealed weapons?
3. Have you ever wondered why you seem to be going on a merry go round of struggles?

CHAPTER 4

Satan's Deceptive Devices

Deceptive devices are everyday life situations that our enemy uses to distract, derail, or deceive us, in an effort to abort us from a life of victory and purpose. The Word of God declares and advises us in 1 Peter 5:8, "Be sober, be vigilant; because your adversary the devil, as a roaring lion, walketh about, and seeking whom he may devour".

In order for us to not only be aware of these deceptive devices, but to defeat them, we must be sober. This means be focused. We have to focus on the fulfilling of our purpose and destiny at any and all costs. We must become mission minded about our assignment. We must be vigilant in pursuit of what God has ordained for our lives. This is not a suggestion, but a command if we are going to be victorious.

The enemy is on assignment every day trying to find ways to devour us. Devour us in our mind, in our actions, in our thoughts, in the words we speak, and devour our faith and belief in God. What do we do when we know an enemy is at hand? We protect ourselves. We protect ourselves by watching and being on guard.

Once you accept that you have an adversary after your destiny, you must protect your destiny. Protect your God-given vision. This can be accomplished through prayer, through reading God's word, and arming yourself spiritually. Ephesians 6:12 advises of this, "For we wrestle not against flesh and blood, but against principalities, against powers, against the rulers of the darkness of this world, against spiritual wickedness in high places".

You must recognize that you are in a fight with your adversary, the devil! He does not want God's purpose to be fulfilled here in earth. He does not want us to operate in a place of victory. When we become defeated in our minds and hearts, we are defeated in accomplishing exploits for God.

Deceptive devices can be confused as normal feelings or emotions. We are faced with many emotions on a daily basis. We live in a society that says go with what you feel. We hear terms such as "it is what it is" and "I feel what I feel", which validates us to go with our feelings. Feelings are normal and a part of the human experience, but unchecked feelings can lead to emotional decisions. Emotional decisions are not a good, because emotions are fleeting and can change from moment to moment.

Christian believers should always operate from a place of truth. You may be asking what truth is. John 17:17 says, "Sanctify them through thy truth: thy word is truth". Yes, you read correctly, the Word of God is what is true. This means that you or I may feel a certain way about a certain situation or issue, but what we feel or think does not mean it is truth. The Word of God is guide to what is true. There are times when we encounter negative situations, and we are tempted to go with what we feel, but we should always strive to go with the truth of God's word even if the situation doesn't look good!

Deceptive devices come to take us further away from trusting and believing in God. Deceptive devices cripple us from walking in the purpose of God for our lives. Deceptive devices are often concealed within the issues and cares of life, which make it hard to detect the deception. Deceptive devices are embedded in our everyday problems. Here are some deceptive devices that I have encountered and wrestled with at one time or another.

Deceptive Device #1:
Fear

I had so much personal failure in my life that I began to fear I would die an "unfulfilled failure". This fear began to cripple me. I couldn't fathom trying to find my purpose because I was so focused on my perceived personal failures. As I shared with you previously, I was a single mother with financial problems, I had a son with a learning disability, I had no romantic relationship, my relationship with my father was not good, and as a result, I began to fear that God had forgot about me. I got to a point where I couldn't dream, and I couldn't plan for a future I was not too sure that I would have. Fear had me bound. I was afraid to try do anything because I feared failure. Do you see what happened? Fear begets fear. Once this deceptive device operates in your life, it only opens the door to more fear. Fear is binding and crippling. More times than not, out fears are unfounded and have no true merit. Who said I had no future? Who said I had no purpose? Who said my life was a failure? Those seeds which were planted by the enemy, seemingly validated by my life circumstances and issues, and I watered them by agreeing with this deceptive device. Fear dominated my life for many years and I didn't even realize it. God's word is truth, and it says, "Fear thou not;

for I am with thee: be not dismayed; for I am thy God: I will strengthen thee; yea, I will help thee; yea, I will uphold thee with the right hand of my righteousness" (Isaiah 41:10).

Deceptive Device #2: Unbelief

Due to the struggles and hardships that I endured, I began to walk in unbelief. I was molested and dealt with so much rejection from childhood to my adult years that once again, I didn't believe God cared for me. Every negative circumstance drove that point home in my heart over and over again. It is impossible to believe God for anything when you have unbelief in your heart. According to James 1:8, "A double minded man is unstable in all his ways". I was double minded in my prayers, I prayed for the things I wanted, but in the back of my mind I didn't necessarily believe God would do it for me. I had many unanswered prayers because of my double minded thinking. I didn't believe God had any purpose for me, I didn't really believe God loved and favored me. I always knew that God had the power to do anything, but as I stated before, I didn't believe He would do it for me.

Deceptive Device #3: Doubt

For a long time, I lived a life of doubt. I doubted that anything good would happen for me. I was simply existing. I didn't have the faith to believe that God had purpose for me. If I heard messages and prophetic words, I doubted that God's word was applicable to my particular situation. I doubted everything and became very negative about everything. I didn't have the faith to believe that God would change my situations. I couldn't believe that goodness could really be present in my life. I spent most of my twenties with a doubtful mindset. I was on a rollercoaster of negative experiences because I didn't believe much of anything. If you're in this place, remember Mark 11:23, "For verily I say unto you, that whosoever shall say unto this mountain, 'Be thou removed, and be thou cast into the sea'; and shall not doubt in his heart, but shall believe that those things which he saith shall come to pass; he shall have whatsoever he saith".

Deceptive Device #4:
Hopelessness

I encountered so much rejection, being ridiculed, personal failures, and past unresolved issues until I became overwhelmed. I was hopeless, and this led to one suicide attempt at the age of 12 and suicidal thoughts on my 29th birthday. I felt as if there was no hope and I was destined to be nobody. At the age of 12, dealing with constant ridiculing, dealing with the effects of molestation, and other issues I felt that suicide was my only option. Both of these times in my life I felt a hopeless despair. Many people have been to this point in life and have committed suicide. Suicide is not the answer, as long as you have breath in your body, your life can change. I thank God that He did not allow the enemy to win. Always take the time to pray for those who may be feeling hopeless. Prayer changes things. The truth of God's word for hopelessness is found in Psalms 31:24, "Be of good courage, and He shall strengthen your heart, all ye that hope in the Lord".

Deceptive Device #5:
Defeat

I felt defeated. I accepted that God didn't really have any purpose. I began to embrace that my only role in life was to support and celebrate others. I began to accept that my life was the way it was and God destined it that way. This defeat took me to a place of depression. I was saddened by the state of my life and thinking I had no future. Depression took me to a dark place for years. I was depressed when I woke up in the morning, depressed at work, depressed at church, and depressed while taking care of my son. Depression is not always identifiable to the untrained eye. I am sure most people that I encountered had no idea of the inner turmoil I carried with me daily. I didn't even realize how depressed I was until one day I realized I had no more dreams. I had nothing else to believe in and nothing to look forward to. I now know that God's Word says, "We are troubled on every side, yet not distressed; we are perplexed, but not in despair; persecuted, but not forsaken; cast down, but not destroyed" (2 Corinthians 4:8-9).

Defeated mindset = no victory!

Deceptive Device #6: Obscured View

My views on life became obscured. I saw God as a big powerful God who could do anything, but I thought He was angry with me all the time based on the things that happened to me. I allowed my life circumstances to become bigger than God. I focused so much on my problems that I couldn't properly focus on the problem solver. I allowed my view to become limited to the possibilities in life. I'm challenging you to look beyond your circumstances. Know that there is more to life than what you are going through. The antidote to an obscured view is found in Psalms 121:

1 I will lift up mine eyes unto the hills, from whence cometh my help. 2 My help cometh from the Lord, which made heaven and earth. 3 He will not suffer thy foot to be moved: he that keepeth thee will not slumber. 4 Behold, he that keepeth Israel shall neither slumber nor sleep. 5 The Lord is thy keeper: the Lord is thy shade upon thy right hand. 6 The sun shall not smite thee by day, nor the moon by night. 7 The Lord shall preserve thee from all evil: he shall preserve thy soul. 8 The Lord shall preserve thy going out and thy coming in from this time forth, and even for evermore.

Deceptive Device #7: Weariness

I became weary in the struggles of life and went into survival mode for most of my adult life. I was tired and didn't have the strength to dream or expect anything from God other than to wake up, go to work, and take care of my son, and attend church. This became my routine for many years. Mental drain causes weariness. When you become weary you are in survival mode and only do what is required. This is counteractive to pursuing purpose, which requires doing more than just what is required of us. Purpose requires showing up and putting in the work. The truth of God's word is found in Galatians 6:9, "And let us not be weary in well doing: for in due season we shall reap, if we faint not".

Those are just a few deceptive devices that I have shared. There are many more. Deceptive devices are given access to our life through normal problems that we all encounter. Giving into our feelings instead of standing on the truth of God's Word gives open access to these deceptive devices. I was going through so many issues and problems, that I took my focus off of the Word of God. I became a person who was validated by my feelings. The truth of the matter is feelings are not always right. There are times we feel offended, but there has been no true offense. How many times have we encountered a situation where we felt that we were the object of conversation, only to find out that was not true? Think about a time where you felt one way, only to find out that you were wrong. This is the problem with trusting our feelings.

If you can take all of the deceptive devices I talked about and imagine one person walking around feeling this way, you can imagine the inner turmoil I felt. I can honestly say I carried deceptive devices in my heart for more than twenty years without realizing the damage it was causing me.

There are no do overs in life, only lessons, so I cannot change my experiences. Now, I will just advise every individual to stay focused, be on guard, and most of all combat every negative feeling with the word of God.

Prayer Changed Me

We can win through prayer. Praying allows the release of burdens. In Matthew 11:30 Jesus said, "For my yoke is easy, and my burden is light". When we pray, we voice our concerns and cares to God. 1 Peter 5:7 says, "Casting all your care upon him; for He careth for you". God cares for us. He cares about what concerns us. An active prayer life allows us to cast our cares upon the Lord, which causes the burdens of our heart to be light. When we are in constant communion with God, we are not so quick to fall into the snare of deceptive devices.

My prayer life suffered for many years because of the things I pondered and meditated on in my heart. You can't entertain negativity and be in the presence of God. Light and darkness have no fellowship.

I cannot stress to you enough the important of knowing God's Word. It is our weapon. When we know what God says, then we know if we experience anything contrary to His word that it is not of Him. It is really that simple. We will encounter life issues, negative issues, bad experiences, and much more, but when we truly understand that God's Word is our truth in every situation, that is when we will gain the victory. Develop a hunger and thirst for the word of God. If you don't have one, don't be afraid to ask God to give it to you and He will do just that.

From today on, no matter what you encounter, stand on the truth of God's Word. Don't allow the cares of life to hide your view of the plans God has for your life. Know that God loves you and He cares for you. Know that God is right there with you. See beyond what you are going through. No matter what is in front of you, God is greater. The plans and purpose He has for you supersedes anything that life throws your way.

Questions to Ponder

1. Take inventory and see if there are any deceptive devices that are ruling your life unaware. If so, list them on a sheet of paper or journal. Now study the Word of God and find a scripture that pertains to what you are encountering. Meditate on the Word and keep it in your heart. Guard with the truth of God's Word.

CHAPTER 5

God's Plan for You and I

I have shared a lot thus far. I have shared about the of issues that I encountered, but the one thing that was really crippling me is that I didn't really know the Word of God for my life. A life without a personal relationship with God lead me to have many wilderness experiences. The wilderness experiences I encountered were not only because I did not know the Word of God, but additionally, my thought process had become tainted and I was unable to come to faith.

How could I follow God if I didn't truly know Him? It was very difficult because I was praying without believing, and if I mustered up enough faith to believe, I soon reverted back to my old mindset because I allowed my circumstances to dictate my level of belief and faith.

I was living a life with a form of godliness but denying the power thereof! Praying and casting my cares on God, but not truly believing in His power to turn the darkest, dire situations around. Can you see the merry go round that I was on? If we are going to pray, we can't worry. If we are going to worry, why pray?

The Bible declares in Hosea 4:6 "My people are destroyed for lack of knowledge: because thou hast rejected knowledge, I will also reject thee, that thou shalt be no priest to me: seeing thou hast forgotten the law of thy God, I will also forget thy children". God was speaking to the people of that time, but it still holds true today. Don't believe me? In Proverbs 29:18 it states, "Where there is no vision, the people perish: but he that keepeth the law, happy is he". I was slowly dying a spiritual death, and I was very unhappy because I had no vision for my life. I simply stopped dreaming or believing for anything and found myself just taking "life" as it came.

If there is no true communion with God, how can we have a vision and knowledge of what God wants from us? Simply put, we cannot. We will attempt to maneuver through our own limited strengths and abilities. Storms are inevitable in everyone's life. The storms that I encountered did not come to break or destroy me, but rather to test, to prove, and to reveal things about me that I did not know. The storms revealed areas of weakness in my life, but also became a testimony to the strength and power of God working in my life even when I didn't realize it.

How did God's plan for my life become hidden? God's plan for me became hidden when I took my focus off of God and put it on myself and what I was going through. I spent so much time consumed and wrapped up in all of the negative circumstances that were happening in my life, that I allowed my circumstances to become my idol. Yes, I said idol. Anything that you spend time thinking about and concentrating on more than God, becomes an idol. My situations became an idol I ate and drank day and night. Oh, I would find time to pray, but I was taking my cares back after prayer, never fully giving them over to God. If I had a true understanding of 1 Peter 5:7 at that time, I would have realized that I had to not only cast my cares to Lord, but I needed to leave them there and not take them back. You may be wondering how you can take your cares back. You can take them back when you start to worry over what you supposedly gave to the Lord. When we start to plan how to fix a care that we gave to the Lord, we have taken that care back.

What have you been dealing with that is causing you to hold back on your God-given purpose?

Are you dealing with any of these blockers below? If so, you'll see what God says about it.

Fear

Fear of failure, fear of success, fear that God has forgotten about you. Fear comes to paralyze not only our actions, but our thoughts and beliefs. In Isaiah 41:10 God says, "Fear not for I am with thee, be not dismayed for I am thy God, I will strengthen thee, I will help thee, and I will uphold thee with the right hand of my righteousness". You are not alone, God is here with us to get us through everything in life that we encounter. Many, including myself, have allowed fear to stop us. Know that God wants us to succeed. He wants us to prosper in the things that He has given us to do.

Trouble

Psalms 46:1 -"God is a very present help in the time of trouble"- A very present help does not mean that we can alter the timing that God chooses to deliver us, but rather we can take comfort in that He is a very real help in the times of trouble. Sometimes the trouble is not removed, but God will give us peace and a calm spirit as we navigate through the choppy, turbulent waters of life.

God never promised that there would not be trouble, but He promised to be with us to the end.

Hopelessness

Perhaps you have been like me and have sunk into depression thinking that you are too far gone or there is no hope for you. Philippians 1:6 says, "He that has begun a good work in you is faithful to perform it to that day". In other words, no matter what has happened or has not happened yet, God will not give up on you and the good work HE has called you to! It is not too late!

Depression

Depression robbed me of having any joy in my life. Any moments of joy I felt, I allowed depression to overshadow those moments. In Nehemiah 8:10 we are told that the joy of the Lord is our strength. So, when we allow or fall into depression, we are sapped of strength. No strength means no energy. No energy leads to laziness and lethargy. There is no drive to do more or be more when joy is absent. Many Christians today are dealing with depression unaware. If you are experiencing a draining sadness in your life that has depleted your energy, you may have fallen into depression. You have to pray against depression and allow God to give you joy. Joy is not the same as happiness. *Happiness* is circumstantial. It depends on the situation as to whether there will be feelings of happiness. *Joy* is contentment even in adverse or unpleasant circumstances. Joy is God-given, it cannot be manufactured.

God's Plans for You and I

Jeremiah 29:11 states that God has good plans for us. Stop thinking you are being picked on, mistreated, or even abused by the situations that you go through. Whether or not you see yourself as an ambassador for Christ on a mission for our Lord, God chose you because He has more confidence in us than we do. We often see ourselves from a victim perspective, when God sees us as the victor or the champion.

God's desire for us is this, "I wish above all things that thou mayest prosper and be in health, even as thy soul prospereth", according to 3 John 1:2. Our heavenly Father not only has great plans for us, but His desire is for us to prosper and be in good health, all while our soul is prospering. What an amazing God we serve! This is His desire for His precious children. Perhaps, you have encountered some storms and problems that made you think contrary to what God says. This is where the fight is, when what we see is not lining up with what God says. In these moments, we are to believe God over our feelings and emotions.

No matter what we are faced with, no matter how many setbacks or losses, Romans 8:28 lets us know, "And we know all things work together for the good of them who love the Lord and who are called according to His purpose".

In this Christian walk, we will face many different trials, issues, and dilemmas, however, Psalms 34:19 promises us that, "Many are the afflictions of the righteous man, but God shall deliver Him out of them all". Everything has a start and an expiration date, it shall not last and God has promised to deliver us out of ALL we go through.

Our attitude should be that of our brother Job. According to the Bible, Job was an upright man. This lets us know that bad things happen to good people too. Job went through some things that if most of us would go through them today, we would curse God and die. In the same day Job lost his wife, his livestock, his children, and his health and his response to it all was to trust God. He said these words, "Though He slay me, yet will I trust Him" (Job 13:15) and "All the days of my appointed time, I'm going to wait until my change comes" (Job 14:14b).

Job knew God through *relationship* and although he was suffering almost beyond human imagination, he didn't curse God, instead he trusted God through it all. Job didn't know we would be reading about his life over 2000 years later, he just knew he was to put his trust and faith in God.

You never know how your faith in God will impact others. Generations to come may read about your life one day and they'll see how you lifted and magnified the name of the Lord no matter what!

How to Overcome

In order to overcome, we must first realize that we have overcoming tools. When these tools are properly applied, they will unlock the doors of joy, prosperity, greater faith, and a relationship with God. The possibilities become endless when we arm ourselves.

One of the best things we can do when we pray is to ask God for a hunger and thirst not only for righteousness, but a hunger and a thirst for knowing His Word. This has been my personal prayer and it has truly increased my desire to know the Word of God for myself. God put a desire in you to truly know His word. This desire will drive you to personal Bible study times and reading other books that can increase your knowledge of God's word.

Simply believe! Belief is a choice. We can either choose to believe or not to believe. There is no in between on the matter. Either we believe what God says which guarantees victory, or we go with our fleeting, fickle emotions, which are based on the current circumstances or situations we find ourselves in. Believe that God put special treasures on the inside of you and believe that God has purpose for your life. Have faith in God. Remember, Hebrews 11:6 states, "But without faith it is impossible to please him: for he that cometh to God must believe that he is, and that he is a rewarder of them that diligently seek him".

Change your mindset, change how you see yourself. We have to change our perspective about the things that we go through in life. The Word declares that He will never put more on us than we can bear. According to Romans 8:37 "Nay in all these things, we are more than conquerors through Him that loved us"—We are conquerors, no matter what we have lost, no matter how many times we have failed, we are more than conquerors through God who loves us. You can't be a failure and more than a conqueror at the same time. What would life be like if you saw yourself as a conqueror?

Prayer

Know that prayer is the vehicle to communicating with God. Not just falling on our knees and saying what we need to say to God, but also listening for Him to speak back. He speaks to us in different ways. Some hear Him audibly, others have an impression or fluttering feeling when God is giving them direction, others hear Him through the word of God, some hear Him through a song, some through visions, others through dreams. As you can see, there is more than one way to hear from God. He speaks to each individual in various manners. It is up to us to build our relationship with Him and find out how He speaks to us. God desires to have communion and fellowship with us. He is always there, always listening, always ready to provide answers and solutions, always there to provide comfort, and always ready to show us His love. We simply have to listen. Psalms 102:17 states, "He will regard the prayer of the destitute, and not despise their prayer". Matthew 21:22 says, "And all things, whatsoever ye shall ask in prayer, believing, ye shall receive". 1 Peter 3:12 says, "For the eyes of the Lord are over the righteous, and his ears are open unto their prayers: but the face of the Lord is against them that do evil". God longs to hear from His children.

Questions to Ponder

1. What are God's plans for your life? If you know them, then write them down.

2. If you do not know God's plan for your life, what steps are you going to take to find out?

CHAPTER 6

Hidden in Plain Sight

H ave you ever torn your house or bedroom up looking for a certain item, only to find that it was hidden right in plain sight? You realize that the very thing you were searching for had been right in front of you the whole time? I refer to this experience as a "duh" moment. If you were a child in the 80's, it's likely that you are very familiar with this term. In case you're not, let me explain. "Duh" was a common term used when someone seemingly didn't know something that they should have known all along. This is how we can feel when we discover that our gifts, talents, treasures, and even our purpose has been in plain sight like the lost item we spent hours searching for. It is my prayer that just like you've found an item in plain sight in your room, likewise, you will identify your hidden treasures and see that your gifts have been near and dear to you your whole life. This chapter will help you clear the clutter and sift through life's circumstances to discover what has become hidden along your journey.

Like me, it is possible that you could have spent years downing yourself and thinking that God forgot to endow you with gifts, when you have been walking in your gifts all along. Many times, we just consider ourselves doing what we do, not realizing we are operating in our purpose.

The truth of the matter is, gifts and talents are usually things that we already do in our everyday lives without realizing the value in it. As you read this chapter, ask God to open up your spiritual eyesight so that you may see the gifts He has placed inside of you. Most times gifts, talents, callings and purpose are in plain sight, but we must look with our spiritual eyes. Spiritual eyes can only be developed through a relationship with God. As you read, I encourage you to look at your life with a new perspective. Our heavenly Father has not forgotten about you! He has deposited amazing treasures inside of you that the world is anxiously awaiting to be revealed all the more.

Know that God did not design your discovery process to be a difficult task, rather He designed it to be purposeful. Everyone's journey to identifying their treasures is going to be different, and there is no one set way to discover your gifts. But, in order for your treasures to be revealed, you must be intentional in your pursuit of God's preordained plan for your life. Purpose, treasure, and destiny will not just simply fall in your lap, you must seek God so that you can come into alignment with His will for your life.

Matthew 6:33 tells us to "Seek ye first the Kingdom of God, and his righteousness; and all these things shall be added unto you". Make no mistake about it, we must pursue God in order to know His plans and His direction for our lives. Notice, the scripture says to seek the Kingdom of God. Much of what we seek today is not Kingdom, but temporal earthly concerns. This is where many have errored. There is nothing wrong with wanting success in our homes, careers, and business endeavors, but we must seek God first. His will must take precedence over any and every plan that we have for our lives. If we believe and follow God's Word, we cannot go wrong. Proverbs 3:5-6 says, "Trust in the LORD with all thine heart; and lean not unto thine own understanding. In all thy ways acknowledge him, and he shall direct thy path".

Purpose is sometimes hidden because we tend to look at things that are more visible. If you are in church, the evangelist, the preacher, and the soloist have what seems to be more visible gifts. When we look a little closer, there are those who may not be in the forefront, but they walk heavily in purpose each and every day.

Have you overlooked your gifts, talents, or purpose because it is not highly visible or easily recognized?

You may not be able to recognize your treasures, but do you know that the people around you can often see your gifts, talents, and purpose even when you can't? I've found this to be true in my life, and this is often validated by our interactions with others. Now, ask yourself, what do people constantly ask of me?

Many people are hard on themselves because they feel they are not walking in purpose, or that they have no gifts and talents. Here are some scenarios for you to consider. Do you see yourself?

The Encourager

Are you an encourager? Do friends and family come to you because you always know what to say and how to encourage their hearts? When people leave your presence, do they always come and back and tell you how much better they felt because they were talking to you?

Have you considered that you have the gift of encouragement? Yes, encouragement is a gift desperately needed in our world, and even more in the body of Christ. Many are discouraged and depressed, dealing with despair or the everyday cares of life. Your gift of encouragement when used properly, can give individuals the boost they need to continue on in their journey with the Lord. Remember, our words have life and the ability to speak hope in dry situations.

The Helper

Do you have the gifts of helps? Are you the person that jumps in where you fit in, no matter the setting? Do you have a knack for just knowing how to do things and when to do them? This is the gift of helps. Many like the spotlight, but the individuals with the gift of helps, work behind the scenes so that things are accomplished. I grew up watching my mom operate in this gift, but I didn't know what it was called. My amazing mom is one of those people who makes things happen. She steps in wherever, and not only does she step in, but she makes things better and her work yields great results. My mom is a "Jill-of-all-trades", she makes flowers, she visits the sick, she supports mothers in labor who ready to give birth, she was a caregiver to my dad, she can raise money like no other, she writes, and she knows the right strategies to make money. There is nothing too big or small for her to get involved with as she willingly works in her gift of helps. This is just a small portion of things she has done over the years. As I stated, to some it may seem as though her gifts weren't easily identifiable because she wasn't an Evangelist, Teacher, Prophet, Pastor, or Apostle, but truly her gift of helps was indeed evident. The gift of helps is needed in order for the church to be successful.

The Counselor

Are you a good listener? Do people come to you in crisis because they know you'll listen without judgement and offer them sound advice? Are you a counselor with no formal training or certification? Do people in your life such as family, co-workers, and friends come to you all the time to talk out a situation in order to gain your perspective? Are you known as a trustworthy person, one who is not a busybody or one who repeats what has been told to them? Wise counsel is a gift. It can be a talent, and it is a treasure. Everyone does not have the ability to give wise counsel. It is not common, so if you possess this type of gift, embrace it and treasure it.

The Intercessor

Do you intercede in your prayer time for others? In your time of prayer, does the Holy Spirit lead you to pray for different people by dropping their names in your spirit; those you don't even know personally? Are you the person praying for people without them even knowing you are praying for them? Are you always praying about situations when you become aware that someone is sick or dealing with an issue? You may be an intercessor. Interceding is a gift, and being an intercessor is a calling. We are to always pray for one another, but an intercessor often intercedes on behalf of others without recognition. Intercessors not only intercede, but their prayers yield results. They can get a prayer through on behalf of others. This type of gift requires an ear to hear God, humility, and discretion. Intercessors may be privy to private situations or even sins that one may be dealing with, by way of the Holy Spirit. This means they have to be trustworthy and discreet. Intercessors are sometimes quiet, reserved individuals who are content in the background, but yet praying in the spirit realm, causing atmospheres to shift and change. Is that you?

The Administrator

Do you have a knack for organization? Do you take care of your family and keep the household organized? Are you the person on the job that just knows what to do? Are you the person in church who plans and knows how to delegate tasks as needed? Do you possess a calm demeanor? Are you a natural born leader? Perhaps, you have the gift of administration.

The gift of administration is a wonderful gift, because we all need organization and structure. Those with the gift of administration usually know how to "declutter". They bring a sense of peace to any situation. Chaos would be rampant if the gift of administration did not exist. The gift of administration operates in executing the "how" of certain tasks. Some people are visionaries but lack the knowledge of how to accomplish the goal. Those with the gift of administration know how to get it done. Can you see how vital this gift is?

The Writer

Are you a really good writer? Are you the person that knows how to effectively articulate ideas on paper? Do you like to research? You may be more of an introvert, but you know how to write well and organize your thoughts on paper. Your words are thought provoking. Writing can be used to speak, used to teach, and even to evangelize. Some people are shy and communicate better via writing. Although we all need to communicate orally, the gift of writing can yield amazing results.

The Teacher

Perhaps you have a way of teaching others that makes learning easy. Are you always offering knowledge and wisdom to those around you without belittling them? Do you have a good understanding of the Bible? Are you a teacher without a degree? Teaching is truly an art form. If you have children, you teach them how to function in society. In your relationships, you teach those you are in covenant with, how to love and treat you. Teaching is a gift. It takes a special person with unique skills to teach Sunday School to children in a way that they understand. I am 46 years old and I can still remember all of my Sunday School teachers. Why? Because they had an effective way to teach me the Word of God and their lessons still have an impact on me today. While at work, are you the person that your co-workers feel free to ask questions because you can teach them without making them feel insignificant or small? Teaching is part of the

Five-Fold ministry gifts (Ephesians 4:11), but it can be used outside of the four walls of the church.

The Coach

Are you the person that your friends come to for advice and direction? Do you coach people through their issues and help them to decide their next steps? Do you cheer people on, helping them experience victory in their life? Could it be that your calling is that of a life coach or spiritual advisor? Spiritual and life coaches have really emerged in the last twenty years. Growing up I never really heard of a coach outside of the sports arena. However, in this day and time, coaches are vital to the success of many. Entrepreneurs are everywhere these days, those who are building a brand or ministry are emerging all the time, and the list goes on and on. People are in need of coaches. Coaches help people go from ideas to implementation. They offer encouragement, support, accountability, assist with plans and help others walk into their destiny. Could you be the person that has been coaching for years with no official name to describe what you have been doing? You can use your coaching skills to build a successful business and your gift can be used for building up others in the body of Christ.

The Soul Winner

Are you an outgoing person that talks to everyone and no one is a stranger? Are you someone who is not afraid to talk to others? Do you have a gift for witnessing and showing the love of God? As believers we are all called to go into the hedges and highways and compel men to come to Jesus, but for *you* this is done with ease. My father was the greatest example of this. He talked to any and everyone at great length. He was never afraid to talk about Jesus or the gospel wherever he went. This included the grocery store, the bank, Walmart, hospitals, nursing homes, jails, and anywhere that he was in the presence of others. This is a gift, and everyone does not possess it to that extent. Are you the one that God gave a natural love for people and a boldness that makes you unafraid? Witnessing and evangelism could be your hidden treasure.

These are just a few gifts that I wanted to share with you. There are so many more found in 1 Corinthians 12. I encourage you to study it at your leisure, but with intentionality as you seek to identify your treasures. There are so many gifts and talents, and God our Father has freely distributed them throughout the body of Christ.

Questions to Ponder

1. What are your specific gifts and talents?
2. Have you identified any gift or talent in this chapter that you are currently walking in? If so, what are they?
3. Has your purpose been hidden in plain sight?
4. Ask a friend or family member what they believe are your strengths or gifts. Take note of their responses. I think you will be pleasantly surprised.

Prayer

"Lord open my eyes and help me to see what you see. Help me to embrace the possibilities that are in front me. Forgive me for thinking that you had forgotten about me. I know now that you have given me treasures. I will actively spend time with you so that they can fully be revealed in my life. Thank you so much for loving me and being patient with me. I believe my treasures are no longer hidden in Jesus name. Amen!"

CHAPTER 7

Hidden Treasures Revealed

I finally came to the realization that there were hidden treasures inside of me. Discovering the hidden treasures that were inside of me was truly a process. As I shared in the last chapter, hidden treasures can be hard to detect, because sometimes they are actually things that come easy to you. It is something that you do without much thought or effort on your part. This is why they can remain hidden for so long because they can be wrapped in everyday normal life routines. As you've read, I found that I was frequently operating in the fruit of my hidden treasures without even realizing it. This may be your experience this too!

Treasures are different from talents. Treasures are for the purpose of the Kingdom. Treasures are precious gifts God gives to His children so that we may operate on His behalf. Talents are also gifts given by God, but talents do not have to be used for the glory of God if the person so desires. Gifts and talents are given without repentance. There are countless talented men and women in the world, but they are not always using their talents for the glory of God. Treasures are precious gifts from God. Treasures are not easily found and require some strategic work to find them.

Hidden treasures are often covered up in dirt and debris. Pearls are found in dirt in the bottom of the ocean. Diamonds are found in black coal. A treasure is something that has to be found and discovered, as it is usually covered in something not so appealing. Sometimes we have to navigate through the muddy unclear waters of life in an effort to find our hidden treasures. Hidden treasures are worth the discovery of them, no matter how painful. They are so precious that once they are found, they have the ability to bring beauty to the life of others.

My life began to change once I became open to the fact that there were some hidden treasures that God had bestowed upon me. I experienced a divine hunger and a realization that there was more than what life had given me. The journey to identifying treasures and purpose is just that; a journey. Journeys are to be enjoyed. Journeys are to be savored as we learn new and glorious things about ourselves and the plans that God has for us.

Have you ever driven on the same interstate, seeing the same scenery each and every time you drive by it, then all of a sudden one day you notice scenery and sights that you somehow overlooked? This is what the journey to purpose is like. Once you become open to the fact that you possess some hidden treasures, you suddenly see things from a different perspective. You are still traveling the same roads, but there is a sensitivity that develops regarding treasures.

As I began to reflect on my life, I found that I had quite a few hidden treasures inside of me that were just waiting to be revealed.

Treasures Concealed Now Revealed

One of the main occurrences that stood out to me was that people have always sought my counsel regarding situations going on in their lives. I was and still am the person among my family and friends that people come to for sound advice. I've been given the gift of wisdom and wise counsel. This is a powerful gift that was not visible to me, but others saw this in me when I didn't see it in myself. My lack of knowledge of the Word of God, didn't allow me to see that this was truly a God-given gift.

I was also the person that people came to for encouragement and to bounce ideas off of. I have always encouraged people without realizing it. Encouragement comes easy to me and it's quite natural. There is nothing fake or phony about the encouragement I am able to give others. People often tell me that I have encouraged them or gave them a great idea for something that they were working on or planning for. This is the gift of coaching. I am a cheerleader for so many individuals; encouraging and supporting them through their personal endeavors with no hidden motives. I do it because it is who I am. I don't do it for personal gain or any type of recompense.

In school, I was always good in English and writing. When I had writing assignments, I realized that I had a knack for writing and was able to do it with ease. I was a person who was good at writing information and sharing it. I was able to capture people's attention because they believed my words were thought provoking. My gift of writing has allowed to me teach on various platforms without any formal training. Currently, I teach and lead a ministry class. I have received many opportunities and invitations to teach what I have created. Additionally, I have written for others. As a licensed evangelist, I believe my treasure of writing will be the most effective form of evangelism for me.

As I've grown older, I've realized that I have the gift of prayer. I never noticed it because I used to pray silently. One day one of my closest friends challenged me to pray out loud. When I prayed out loud, I noticed that I have the ability through the Holy Spirit to make a connection during prayer. I am able to hear through the Holy Spirit what to pray for. I have prayed for many individuals who let me know that my prayers are their heartfelt and secret prayers that they have shared only with the Lord. This is a treasure that everyone does not have.

As I've continued to pursue God, I've found that I am intercessor as well. Intercessors pray for people who they know, but also pray for people they don't know personally. Intercessors intercede on behalf of an individual, family, or situation without being asked. They carry a burden for others that is only relieved through praying with them. There are many times that I pray for people who I don't know personally, some who I know but don't talk to, and others who may not care for me. This is what an intercessor does. An intercessor does not need to make an announcement about how they are praying for you. They simply just pray. Just think, you may have some silent prayer partners that may never reveal themselves to you, though they are constantly interceding for you.

Oftentimes, we become who or what we need in our lives. Life's issues have a way of magnifying what we are missing. Hidden treasures can reveal themselves through those life issues, struggles, and through the tests that we endure.

I was going through so much turmoil and so many issues, that I longed for a friend who gave wise counsel. I looked for others to encourage me. I looked for people who were interceding on behalf without me asking. I started coaching people through their problems because I longed for someone to coach and mentor me as I navigated the storms of life. I became the woman that I needed in my life and I became the friend I wanted to have.

The Bad Working For My Good

As I've mentioned throughout the book, my treasures were overshadowed and hidden. I realize now that all the bad things I experienced were working for my good. Through rejection, molestation, ridicule, and hurt, self-loathing was birthed. I was unable to see that I had anything of worth to offer. For years I dreamed of helping and teaching women, but my own issues had me bound. In addition to dealing with the issues above, I suffered with low self-esteem until I entered my 40's and insecurity would rare its ugly head from time to time. I would not have chosen to experience the pain I had my life, but I don't believe that I would be as sensitive as I am to others if I had not encountered and overcome these struggles.

One of the most traumatic occurrences in my life was being molested. I thought that I didn't deserve a healthy and loving relationship because of the molestation that I experienced. Molestation is typically done in the dark and in secret. As a result, I believed the lie that I was not good enough to be loved openly and freely; therefore in future relationships, I settled when I should have expected and demanded more. Some effects of molestation include feelings of guilt and shame. Oftentimes, victims of molestation believe that they somehow deserved what happened to them, and this is exactly how I felt. This guilt carried over into my relationships, causing me to blame myself for problems that would arise. If you've been molested and have felt this way, none of this is true, it is all deception. The *truth* is that if you have experienced molestation, rape, or have been violated in any way, you <u>did not</u> deserve what happened to you. The person who hurt you had the problem. In order to heal effectively, the following steps are essential: recognize that you didn't deserve to be violated, forgive the perpetrator even if they never apologize, pray for their healing and deliverance, and seek counseling if you need it. The process of healing is not easy, but it's necessary so that you can be free instead of bound by what happened to you. Although the molestation was difficult to deal with, if I would not have gone through it, I wouldn't be able to encourage others who have gone through the same thing. Because I know firsthand how molestation impacts lives, I am now able to effectively edify women, helping them recognize their worth in spite of what they have been through.

After the Reveal

Once I began to identify my hidden treasures, that was only the beginning of my continued quest. There was always a longing inside me that wouldn't allow me to quit. I knew that there was something more for me, but I was unsure how I was going to find it. Now that I knew there was so much inside of me, I knew I needed more.

I started to read a variety of books. I went to a lot of women's conferences, programs, and supported so many women-of-action as I tried to figure out what my treasures truly were. I dared not speak out to anyone all that God began to show me, but slowly on the inside I was healing. My self-esteem started to pick up. I finally felt that I had purpose. That is the best validation you can ever receive. When God bestows gifts and treasures inside of you, your self- esteem will soar!

I finally saw all that I was. As social media become prevalent, I finally saw individuals who shared some of the same treasures that I had in me and I was able to put a title to who I really was. A spiritual life coach. I am a speaker. I am a counselor. I am a writer. I am an evangelist. I am an intercessor. I savored these treasures for years before I began the process of becoming all that I was and am supposed to be.

I can't believe I spent most of my life thinking I had nothing of significance to offer, only to discover that God had been more than generous with the treasures He placed on the inside of me. I discovered that God thought more about me than I did myself! Do you *really* realize how much God loves you? I hope you are beginning to understand how much He has invested in you? God is calling you to carry out His mission through the treasures He has placed inside of you.

God is so amazing! He really does use what the enemy meant for evil, for our good! What was meant to permanently silence me, destroy me, and kill me, God is now using to help others who are going through what I have overcome! To God be the glory! What an amazing plan.

You have a story too! God using your bad for your good and for His glory. He gets the glory when we tell the whole story. Someone is waiting to hear and experience the treasures that God has placed in you. How much longer will you allow treasures to be undiscovered?

It is way past the time to allow those hidden treasures to be revealed!

Questions to Ponder

1. What do people often seek for your assistance with?
2. Think about painful situations that have occurred in your life. How can you help others overcome in that area as well?

CHAPTER 8

I Can See Clearly Now

Once I realized the treasures that God had indeed placed on the inside of me, it was as if the mist and the fog suddenly rolled away and my vision became crystal clear. I began to see not only the treasures, but I began to see what could become if I truly allowed God to have *total* control of my life. I went from *no* vision, to *possibilities*, to *vision* for my life.

Years of wrong thinking, years of agreeing with the enemy of my soul, and years of low self-esteem came to a screeching halt! I started seeing that God was going to use my life to be a testimony to someone about His delivering power, His saving grace, and His power to raise you up despite what you have been through.

Studying the Word of God allowed me to see God in a different light. I began to see that He is indeed a loving God, who allows us to go through things not to hurt us, but to grow and expand us all for His purpose. Throughout the Bible there are a number of individuals who faced much opposition but were victorious because of their unwavering faith and trust in God. Ponder this for a moment: when we are reading the Bible, we are reading in past tense. We are able to see the purpose and end result of a story. So, when we are studying the Word, we should be able to clearly see that God was not punishing individuals who had to walk through hard trials. He was molding and making them for His purpose and glory. Reading the Word of God allows us to know God and how He brings us through.

Focus on the Promise

Consider the children of Israel, God was simply trying to deliver them from slavery and bring them to the Promised Land. Nowhere in the story do we see God trying to afflict, hurt, or cause pain to the children of Israel. They began to murmur and complain because they encountered things that they had not encountered before. They were put in a position where they had to trust God and rely on Him to not only lead them, but also to feed them daily. They could not rely on the slavery system that they were accustomed to, they had to rely on God. Numbers 14:2 states, "And all the children of Israel murmured against Moses and against Aaron: and the whole congregation said unto them, 'If only we would have died in the land of Egypt! Or if we would God we had died in this wilderness".

You may ask, "Why would they want to go back to slavery and bondage"? It was because it was what they were used to. Sometimes God is trying to bring us to our greater destiny and we cling to what is familiar even when it bad for us. Trusting and relying on God became a chore for them and their eyes began to focus on the problems rather than the promise. Have you been like the Israelites murmuring and unable to see God's bigger plan? Complaining is a dangerous game. The Apostle Paul instructs us to be content in whatever state we are in. Philippians 4:12 says, "I know both how to be abased, and I know how to abound: everywhere and in all things I am instructed both to be full and to be hungry, both to abound and to suffer need". This means in whatever state we are in, we will not complain.

Many of us have encountered wilderness experiences. Wilderness experiences come as a result of not trusting God and leaning on our own understanding. Proverbs 3:5 instructs us to, "Trust in the LORD with all thine heart;

and lean not unto thine own understanding. In all thy ways acknowledge him, and he shall direct thy paths". When we encounter an abundance of issues and problems, we can find ourselves leaning and depending on what we understand. This is the wrong way to think. Always trust God and His plan even when you don't quite understand all that He is doing. Our Father always knows best!

God uses our life struggles, issues, and trials to draw us closer to Him, to reveal who He is, and to reveal what He has put in us. Once we begin to understand His purpose for allowing some of the things we go through, it allows us to go through with the right attitude.

In my early 30's I finally began to see how the enemy had distorted my perception of God and His love for me. I began to see that God is not a respecter of persons, but everyone has a different path to take in order for them to reach the people they are called to in this life. We all cannot take the same journey. Don't make the mistake of thinking that just because someone has not encountered what you have encountered, or that because you are unable to see what they are dealing with, that they haven't gone through anything, or that God favors them more. That is another lie from enemy.

God needs His people to be a witness in every path of life. In other words, everyone will take different paths in life based on whatever the purpose and plan that God has chosen for them. We will all encounter different situations and struggles, but it is all for the glory of God to be revealed through each and every situation. There are people who encounter inner struggles that may never be public, but daily they are fighting private battles. There are individuals who deal with rage, unforgiveness, hatred, envy, bitterness, low self-esteem, brokenness and this list goes on and on. These are some inner battles that are often masked, but they're strong enough to keep an individual from functioning in the purpose and plan of God for their life. Just remember you may never know what a person encounters, but just know that everyone is fighting some type of battle.

There are people who will walk a path with seemingly countless public battles. They have encountered various mess-ups, have made many mistakes, people who may have been molested or abused, people who have dealt with multiple unsuccessful marriages, people who have had abortions, drug addicts, prostitutes, and the list goes on and on. These individuals are often called to other individuals like themselves who have encountered some of these same problems. It is never about us! What we encounter is always to help someone else.

These different kinds of situations come to show the power of God. The power of God to heal, the power of God to deliver, the power of God to breaks the bonds of oppression and addiction, the power of God that forgives us our sins, the power of God to raise people up to be great men and women of God. Can you see the glory of God being revealed in the lives of these types of individuals? It is indeed powerful, and their testimonies give life and hope to the hopeless.

Know that every walk of life is necessary for the glory of God to be revealed. It is God who makes the choice on who encounters what in life. Remember, God often has more confidence in what He has instilled in us than we do. He sees what we don't see. He knows what you were created for and what your tolerance and endurance level is. Imagine what would happen if you looked at the difficulty and trials in your life from the viewpoint that *God has so much confidence in me that He is allowing me to go through this.* What if we become more determined to make our "Daddy" (*Heavenly Father*) proud of us during the hard times and difficulties assigned to us? I challenge you to change your perspective in order to win.

Be assured that the people that you are called to will identify with your life. The people that you are called to will see themselves through your story, through your ministry or simply through your conversation. As you uncover your hidden treasures and share them, others will become empowered as they discover their hidden treasures.

I finally began to see that my struggles in life do not dim that I am fearfully and wonderfully made. It does not dim that I am called according to God's purpose. It does not dim that God has good plans for my life. It does not dim the light that God has placed on the inside of me.

The path for my life became clearer. I started to focus more on me and what I am supposed to be. I learned the word "no". "No" is a powerful word. I stopped wasting a lot of time doing things that would not enhance or help my purpose. Now I say "no" to things that do not benefit my purpose. My time is no longer wasted on frivolity. I am about my Father's business.

It is always in order to be helpers one to another, but not to the detriment of not being obedient to God's plan for your life. Some people fall into the trap of assisting others, while ignoring the fact that God has something for them to do as well. Help but don't hinder. Help someone, but don't become a hindrance to your own progress. There is balance for everything that needs to be done. There may even come a season when you can't even assist because your assignment has become bigger and requires all of your attention. That is ok too. As I previously stated, help but don't hinder.

Once you discover your hidden treasures, it's time to fine tune your treasures and expand what God has placed inside of you. This is necessary if you want to truly maximize all that you have. Don't think for one minute that because God gives you treasures and gifts that you don't have to work on them. A true servant seeks to fine tune what has been placed in their hands. How can you fine tune your treasures? Invest in yourself.

Invest in You!

You will have to invest in yourself and your hidden treasures that are now revealed. Investing in yourself is not always money; it can include time, dedication and sacrifice. The internet has a plethora of information, and a lot of the information is free. There will be times when you will need to make a financial investment, and in those times, remember you are worth it. Don't be afraid to invest in yourself. It is not about splurging on yourself, but it is about being a good steward of what God has given you.

By nature, I support people in their endeavors, but I had to be more strategic about lending my time when I needed to be supporting and growing myself.

For example, because I knew that my gifts matched those of a spiritual life coach, one of the first things I researched on the internet was how become a certified coach. Before I could get to the place of formal training, I had to truly believe that this was my hidden treasure and that I was truly called to help coach others to fulfilling purpose in life.

As I continue to grow, now I am currently in the process of becoming a Christian counselor. I believe that although I have counseled dozens of people, a formal education is a way for me to further invest in what God has given me. Formal education and training help you to become more effective in the services you are providing. Don't be afraid to invest in yourself and the gifts that God has given you.

Although I was a person who wrote with ease, I was still not a published author. I sought out book coaches and programs, and unfortunately, I wasted a lot of money. Some of it was my fault for not truly being one hundred percent vested in the program, but I also needed to find a program that was right for me. Lesson learned. I didn't give up, and finally found the right fit for me which included accountability. Once you discover the right fit or the right person to take you to the next level, things truly begin to flow. I can honestly say that God led me to my book coach and what you are reading today is a result of the right fit! It is out there. I want to encourage someone who may have wasted some money like I did, to keep searching because what you need is out there.

If the smoke has not cleared away as of yet, ask God to clear the smoke so that you can see what He wants you to be. He can give you fresh perspective on your trials and tribulations. He can cause you to see things in His light. Ask God to open your heart, then open your eyes so that you can not only see your hidden treasures but you can hone in them and grow. Jesus said it best, if thou canst believe, all things are possible to him that believeth. If you believe that God has not forgotten you, that God has hidden treasures waiting to be revealed through you, then you can do exploits in His name (Daniel 11:32).

Questions to Ponder

1. If you still don't see clearly, what is blocking your vision?
2. Identify three ways to invest in yourself immediately.

CHAPTER 9

Becoming a True Treasure Seeker

B ecause you've made it this far in the book, prayerfully you have a new awareness regarding hidden treasures. The hidden treasures which have been revealed or confirmed should become your focus! These are the things you are to execute with all that is within you. God has opened your eyes to His plan for your life. He has exposed your hidden treasures. You may have to put in some strategic work, but those hidden treasures have been revealed for a reason. You have been officially charged!

No longer can you say you have no idea, and no longer can you think that God has forgotten about you. No more second guessing what God has placed inside you. It is time to come forth. You are a woman with gifts and treasures. What will you do with them? Your assignment is waiting and the people assigned to you are awaiting you.

It is time to sharpen your skills in the areas of your treasures and gifts. It is time to walk in what God has purposed for your life. Remember, no treasure is too small or insignificant. God can and will use everything that He has gifted you with for His glory if you allow Him to be Lord over your life. Don't waste any more time, get busy as the Bible commands us in 1 Corinthians 15:58, "Therefore, my beloved brethren, be ye steadfast, unmovable, always abounding in the work of the Lord, forasmuch as ye know that your labor is not in vain in the Lord".

You will be challenged, you will be stretched, you will be pulled, and you may even want to halt, but know that the will of God must be done. You must do your part. Let no one and nothing stop you from walking in your purpose and using your treasures. No matter what, stay focused. You can remain focused by following the words found in Psalms 121:1-2, "I will lift mine eyes to hills, from whence cometh my help. My help cometh from the LORD, which made heaven and earth". Keep your eyes on God!

It is time that we come into agreement with all that God has called us to be. Coming into agreement with God does not mean that we understand all that He is doing and it does not mean that the road will be easy. It simply means that you will remain surrendered to God and believe Him even when it's hard to believe. If God says you are a speaker called to the nations, then guess what, that is what you are. It does not matter if you have a speech impediment, it does not matter if you are painfully shy, it does not matter that you don't have the money or education, the only thing that matters is what God says.

God knows what we possess and what we don't possess, He didn't consider any of that when He put His treasures on the inside of you. All God needs is a "Yes"! He will do the rest, each and every time. He will lead and guide us if we step out on the strength of His Word.

Whatever your treasures are, use them to the glory and honor of God. Our Heavenly Father knows what He has invested in us and intends for us to use these gifts and treasures for His glory.

Know that our God is a great big God and He has endless treasures and gifts for His children. I challenge you to not just get comfortable in what you feel you may know about your gifts, but go deeper in the word of God. Go deeper in prayer, God wants to open so much up to us. We have to earnestly seek the Lord according to Deuteronomy 4:29 which states, "But if from thence thou shalt seek the Lord thy God, thou shalt find him, if thou seek him with all thy heart and with all thy soul". In addition, I Chronicles 16:11 advises us to seek the Lord and his strength, seek his face continually.

Mission of a Treasure Seeker

We are going to become treasure seekers. Treasure seekers intentionally seek to discover hidden treasures. Treasure seekers are able to see that each person has some treasures that need to come to life.

I challenge you to change the way you see people. See them as individuals who have some hidden treasures and gifts that God wants to reveal through them. If you notice that a person is not walking in their purpose, see them as someone who may need assistance getting to that place in God. Encouragement costs us nothing. Encourage them through the word of God, kind words of love, and even acts of kindness.

We simply cannot just stop at developing our own treasures and talents and forget about others who are struggling. You must now turn around and ignite your sister or brother on this journey to purpose. There are countless treasures in the Earth waiting to be utilized. Someone somewhere is allowing their hidden treasures to be concealed by life.

A treasure seeker is one who seeks to help others find their hidden treasures. It is our duty to bring them to awareness. We can do this by sharing our journey to finding our hidden treasures. Don't be afraid to share your story of how you discovered your hidden treasures. Perhaps this book was the catalyst for change in your life. Share this information with someone you know who may be struggling with finding and operating in their purpose. Perhaps through your story, someone will find themselves and tap into who God made them to be. The possibilities are endless when we take on the mission to be treasure seekers.

I would ask you to consider how you have felt not really knowing your purpose. Think of the confusion, frustration, and feelings of defeat you experienced at times. Think of how God has shined the light on who He created you to be; now wouldn't you like others to experience the same wonderful revelations? This is why we cannot stop at just working with our treasures, but we must also assist others in coming into this light. How can we leave our sisters and even brothers in the dark, when we now have the answers they have been looking for?

Make it your life mission to help someone along as they journey toward discovering their life's purpose. Remember the Word of God according to 2 Corinthians 4:7, "We have these treasures hidden in earthen vessels that the excellency of the power may be of God, and not of us". This scripture lets us know that everyone has something inside of them just waiting to be revealed.

There are countless people like you and I who desire to identify their treasures. Life has happened to them, their treasures have been concealed, and some people have even put them on the backburner for use at a later date. Individuals have been in prayer for years and have gone to numerous conferences and church services searching for a prophetic word to point them to their purpose. You may be the answer to their secret prayers! Because you've identified your treasures by reading this book, you now hold the keys to help someone unlock their hidden treasures. How awesome is it that God can now use you as a treasure seeker to usher someone into what He has for them! You and I have power to change others' lives!

Let's make a collective declaration that we will not allow another person to die under our watch with unfulfilled purpose and hidden treasures that were never revealed.

Kingdom Minded

Kingdom minded people will do whatever it takes to advance the Kingdom of God. If we become treasure seekers, we will help inspire and influence others to fulfill their God-given purpose. This helps to expand the Kingdom of God. No one person can reach everyone, but collectively, if spirit filled, Bible believing, redeemed people of God would do their part in helping treasures be discovered, then the gospel of Jesus Christ can be spread to each and every corner of this earth. That is a powerful thought!

The atmosphere should be charged with excitement about helping others find their hidden treasures. If we are Bible believers, we know the days are short. We want to be about the Father's business, winning souls, and doing everything we can to further the Kingdom of God. Gladly take on the mission of Christ.

Don't always think you will see a return on your investments in ministry because you will not. There will people whose life you touch and people you have impacted that you may never see again in this life, but just know that seeds are not wasted when we do it for the glory of God.

We are to plant the seeds and let God bring the increase (1 Corinthians 3:6). It's important for us to do good works unto God without expecting a reward and to have pure motives when we help others. Remember God is the one who keeps records and rewards! "Henceforth there is laid up for me a crown of righteousness, which the Lord, the righteous judge, shall give me at that day: and not to me only, but unto all them also that love his appearing" (2 Timothy 4:8).

Questions to Ponder

1. Name some people you know who need assistance with discovering their hidden treasures.

2. What are some ways you can assist them while they're on their journey to discover hidden treasures?

CHAPTER 10

Purpose into Profit

C an you profit from your purpose? The answer is absolutely yes. Walking in purpose does not mean that you cannot profit. Consider this, we are compensated for our skills and abilities on our jobs, so how much more would our heavenly Father allow us to profit from gifts and talents that He Himself has placed on the inside of us.

As Christian believers, we are always called to serve others. Serving others does not always mean that it has to be for free. Now I am in no way suggesting that in every area we find ourselves serving, that we should expect to gain a profit. We ought to have a servant's heart in all that we do. We should be found serving without expecting compensation. I am specifically referring to our service in our churches, communities, and even our families. Your name should not always be attached to a dollar amount. Remember, we are the Lord's hands extended; reaching out to others on His behalf. However, I do want you to consider profiting from some of the hidden treasures that God has released in your life.

For many years there has been a misconception that people in ministry could not profit from the gifts and talents that God has given them. This is a big misconception as the Word of God tells us that it is God who gives us power to get wealth. How do we get wealth? We don't get the kind of wealth that God is referring to simply by working for others. We can be both wealthy naturally as well as spiritually.

Spiritual Wealth

When we walk in purpose, we are wealthy. We become spiritually wealthy when we are in perfect alignment with God's plan for our lives. Being spiritually-wealthy means we are rich in God's word, rich in prayer, rich in communion with God, and rich because we are walking in our purpose. This gain is greater than any financial gain that you or I could ever receive.

Before we discuss ways to profit from your purpose, let's discuss the non-monetary benefits that can be yours when you are walking in purpose. The first and most important benefit is that you are in the perfect will of God and doing what God has purposed you to do. There is no greater satisfaction outside of the feeling you have knowing that you are pleasing God. Imagine laying in your bed at night and reflecting on your day and you realize that everything God assigned you to do that day was completed. What an amazing feeling! No sleeping pill or potion can bring you the sweet rest that comes with knowing that your Heavenly Father is pleased with you! Obedience makes a mighty fine pillow to rest your head on.

Another benefit of walking in purpose is that you are helping others break free, be healed, and get delivered from things that held them back from fulfilling purpose. As a treasure seeker you should be excited to watch someone awaken and walk into purpose. You are not only walking in your own purpose, but you have assisted in the process of someone else walking in their purpose. This is the kind of work that will praise you in the Gates of Heaven.

Natural Wealth

God gives us the power to get wealth according to Deuteronomy 8:18, "But thou shalt remember the Lord thy God: for it is he that giveth thee power to get wealth, that he may establish his covenant which he sware unto thy fathers, as it is this day". If God gives us the power to get wealth, then will He not also provide us with the talents and gifts to gain that wealth? God not only gives us gifts and talents, but He will also give us strategies on how to attain wealth.

Now let us consider the monetary benefits that can be associated with your purpose, passion, and gifts. Some ways we can profit from our treasures include things such as, if we are a speaker, charging a speaker fee. If we are coaching or counseling, we should be compensated. If you have the knowledge and know- how for certain areas and are willing to share the information or train individuals, this is also an opportunity to make a profit.

Suppose you have a gift of cleaning and it is truly your passion. You are quite good at it. This could be your ministry. There are a lot of people who need help cleaning their homes. You can profit by charging a fee to clean their home. Cleaning homes is still considered ministry when you do it to the glory of God, and you can also share the Word of God with those you encounter. You can market your business as a Christian business. You can use discretion as when to charge for cleaning and when not to charge. Let the Holy Spirit guide you. You may be led to intercede for the family while cleaning their home.

What if the home you were cleaning was a home of domestic violence? Do you know that while you are cleaning and praying, demons will have to flee that home? We have to see the bigger picture in all that we do. Prayer is a powerful weapon and it truly changes things. Don't just think that you are cleaning the house but realize that you can do some serious spiritual warfare while cleaning, thus changing the atmosphere of that home.

What if you are a great cook? Folks rave over your food because it is just *that* good. You can turn this into a ministry. No gift is too small or insignificant. God does not waste anything! So, if you are gifted for something, God has given it to you so that you may help others. If you are a great cook, a good way to balance between your purpose and profit, is to charge to cook food for people who desire your food, but also cook and give food to those who may be without. As the Lord's extended hands, when you cook a meal for someone, let them know how God placed them on your heart; this shows them that God is concerned about them and they are on His mind! Give them a meal "on God" through you. This is ministry. Everyone needs to eat, and most of us love to eat, so this ministry can be lucrative!

If you're someone who is creative and good with your hands, there are many doors that your hidden treasures can open for you. This can include being someone who sews well, makes flowers, makes jewelry, does hair, and more. These are all gifts, talents, and hidden treasures that can be used to build the Kingdom of God and cause you to gain wealth. Think about what you have been doing up to this point. Have you been leaving money on the table because you thought your purpose couldn't bring in profit?

Perhaps you are an anointed caregiver, you know how to meet the needs of your patients, you know how to encourage them, or even lighten the burdens that sickness can bring, this may just also be your hidden treasure. Now that you have identified your treasure, use it for the glory of God. You can offer free service in some instances depending on the need, and you can also charge a fee for services. You can even train others on how to be caregivers. There can be a charge for this training or class as caregivers are needed all the time.

Realize that there are countless people on the earth looking for what you possess. The demand is high, so the supply is necessary. In these days and times of uncertainty, fear, and discouragement, people are looking for individuals who can help them to make sense of their lives. We don't have all the answers but in whatever capacity of purpose you operate in, you have the answer if you have Jesus Christ!

Conclusion

As I close, ponder everything that I have shared throughout this book. Know that God created and purposed you for an amazing plan. You were created to contribute to the Kingdom of God. Think about what life may have concealed from you. Think about the hidden treasures that you have discovered since reading this book. Think of the hidden treasures you were operating in already that you may have not been aware of. Know that what God has put in you is going to help others in reach their destiny in God.

Don't despise all the not-so-great moments in your life, know that what the enemy meant for evil God has turned around to use for your good. The weapons formed, but they did not prosper (Isaiah 54:17). You are still standing despite all that came to destroy you. You are still standing by the grace of God because He has great plans for you.

See yourself differently. You are no longer bound by circumstances. You are not a victim, but you're a victor. Whatever happened to you does not define who you are. You are not just a conqueror, but more than a conqueror. Change your perception that God may have been angry with you or that He's punishing you for the wrong you have done in life. Know that He loves you. Yes, sometimes

He chastens us, but He is a loving and merciful God. Lamentations 3:22-23 declares, "It is of the Lord's mercies that we are not consumed, because his compassions fail not. They are new every morning: great is thy faithfulness". Every single morning God gives us new mercy, He is faithful to us even when we are not faithful to Him. He didn't let life consume us because He knew the plans He had for us.

We have the ability to profit and do ministry all at the same time. God is just good like that! If you ask the Lord to give you knowledge on how to run your business, He will do just that. Don't be afraid to ask for wisdom and creativity, it is yours for the asking. You can profit from your treasures and also be a blessing with those same treasures. Ask God to give you a healthy balance of both. Above all do it for the glory of God!

It doesn't matter where you come from, what you have endured, or what you have done. You are good enough. You are anointed. You are beautiful. You are a treasure waiting to be revealed. It is time to shine like a diamond, so that the light of the Lord can be displayed through you. Don't allow the enemy of your soul to win this war he has waged against you. You and I win when we say yes to the Lord, when we agree with His plan for our life, and most importantly, when we obey God. We win!

Questions to Ponder

1. What treasures, gifts and talents do you possess that you could be making a profit from?

2. Are there some opportunities where you can freely give of your gifts and talents? List them below.

Prayer

"Father thank you opening my eyes. Thank you for allowing me to see me as You see me. Thank you for the hidden treasures you have revealed in me. I thank you for loving me and being with me every step of the way. Now God, I commit to You all of my treasures. I acknowledge my treasures, I accept them, and I will be a good steward of them with everything I have on the inside of me. I decree you will get the glory out of my life. I will not shrink back or go back to a place of complacency. I am going to be all that You desire me to be. I am going to reach everyone that You have called me to impact. Thank you for entrusting me with these treasures. I will actively draw close and pursue you so you can lead me. I want to make you proud. I love you forever, in Jesus name, Amen."

Acknowledgments

I want to give honor and praise to my Lord and Savior, Jesus Christ. I thank you Lord for loving me, for calling me, for putting purpose in me. I thank you for never giving up on me. I thank you for being faithful to me when I was not faithful to you. I thank you Father for the hidden treasures you allowed to be revealed in me. My sole desire is to please you and do all that you have commanded me to do. I love you Lord with my whole heart, mind, body, and spirit.

I want to acknowledge my beautiful Mother, Mable Beckett. Your unwavering support, unconditional love, wisdom, and sacrifices down through the years cannot ever be repaid. I thank you for always encouraging and pushing me to do what God has destined me to do. You are an example of love, servitude, and faith. You have shown me how to put my trust in God. You have shown me what it is to be a woman and a Mother. I am so thankful for everything you have done in my life. Words cannot express my gratitude.

I want to acknowledge my wonderful son PJ; being your Mom has been the best thing that I have ever done.

You are the epitome of the perfect son. I love you so much and I thank God that He entrusted you to me. I love you for never complaining in the lean times. I thank you for pushing me to write. I thank you for the support and prayers that you have provided me with. The best is yet to come for you, son!

I want to acknowledge my brothers and sisters. We are family and I love each and every one of you. Denise, Gerald, Orlando, John, Ronnie (RIP), Bruce, Robert, Angie, and last but not least, Robin. You all have taught me that the love of family can sustain us through any and everything we can encounter in life.

I thank God for my upbringing in New Jerusalem Church of God in Christ. I thank God for my late Pastor, Bishop B.K. Thoroughgood (Lady Ernestine). I thank you for teaching me the ways of holiness and serving God in a spirit of excellence. You left me with such a strong foundation and legacy, and for that, I am eternally grateful. I am rooted and grounded in God because of what you imparted into my life.

I honor my late Pastor, Elder Adam L. Thourogood, Sr. (Lady Charmyn). You were a true brother, Pastor and friend. Although your time of serving as Pastor was too short, it was the most impactful time in my life. I thank you for the lessons on love, forgiveness, and maintaining the standards of holiness. Thank you for believing in me and allowing me to serve my childhood friends who became my leaders. I will always look back on those days with joy in my heart.

To my current Pastor Dr. Yd Thoroughgood (Lady Shylene), you have shown me how to be resilient when faced with the storms of life. You have the heart of a servant and a heart for the people of God. Through your perseverance, I have learned that there are no excuses when it comes to serving God and doing what we are called to do. I am grateful for these powerful lessons. May God continue to strengthen you and give you long life!

To Chantel, you are my best friend. Thank you for being my sounding board and listening ear. You have always encouraged me to write my book and share my life stories. You always saw more in me than I saw in myself. You have encouraged me when I didn't think I could go any further. You have kept my secrets. Thank you for the laughs, the love, the talks, the crying sessions, and crab leg feasts (lol). I love you to life my sister, my friend.

I thank God for my New Jerusalem Church of God in Christ church family. We have weathered the storms of losing two of our beloved Pastors unexpectedly, but yet remained a strong church family. I am grateful for the praying women of our church. We are one!

I have made so many wonderful friends down through the years. There are way too many to name individually, but the bond of sisterhood and love remains the same. I love you all forever.

I want to publicly thank you, Yvette Thoroughgood, for being a true confidant. I have been able to share all of my goals as it relates to my purpose. You have kept it all confidential. You have read my unedited writings, sermon notes, and have always provided encouragement and positive feedback. Thank you for being a woman of integrity and great character.

I want to thank my book coach and publisher, Mrs. Teresa R. Hunt. You were sent by God to guide me through the process of writing and publishing this book. I am grateful for your professionalism, dedication, and your commitment to excellence.

To every reader, I thank you for your support. Know that you are appreciated and loved. Thank you.

About the Author

 Michelle Beckett is a woman on a mission to fulfill God's purpose and plan in her life. As a licensed Evangelist and a Certified Spiritual Life Coach, her calling is to help women discover their hidden treasures through the Word of God. Michelle is passionate about encouraging others through acts of kindness and giving wise counsel. She can often be found teaching women practical life tips and mentoring young ladies. Michelle holds an A.A.S degree in Medical Reimbursement and Coding from Bryant and Stratton College. She is currently pursuing formal training in the area of Christian counseling. Michelle is a trained speaker through the Emerge Academy and she speaks at women's conferences, revivals, and services. Her greatest accomplishment is raising her wonderful son. Michelle's favorite scripture is Romans 8:28 "And we know all things work together for the good of them who love the Lord and are called according to His purpose".

Made in the USA
Middletown, DE
13 August 2018